Dirty Work

DIRTY TRUE CRIME JOBS

Kenny Abdo

Fly!
An Imprint of Abdo Zoom
abdobooks.com

abdobooks.com

Published by Abdo Zoom, a division of ABDO, P.O. Box 398166, Minneapolis, Minnesota 55439. Copyright © 2026 by Abdo Consulting Group, Inc. International copyrights reserved in all countries. No part of this book may be reproduced in any form without written permission from the publisher. Fly!™ is a trademark and logo of Abdo Zoom.

Printed in the United States of America, North Mankato, Minnesota.
052025
092025

THIS BOOK CONTAINS RECYCLED MATERIALS

Photo Credits: Alamy, AP Images, Getty Images, Shutterstock
Production Contributors: Kenny Abdo, Jennie Forsberg, Grace Hansen
Design Contributors: Candice Keimig, Neil Klinepier, Colleen McLaren

Library of Congress Control Number: 2024947688

Publisher's Cataloging-in-Publication Data

Names: Abdo, Kenny, author.
Title: Dirty true crime jobs / by Kenny Abdo
Description: Minneapolis, Minnesota : Abdo Zoom, 2026 | Series: Dirty work | Includes online resources and index.
Identifiers: ISBN 9781098288747 (lib. bdg.) | ISBN 9781098289447 (ebook) | ISBN 9781098289799 (Read-to-me ebook)
Subjects: LCSH: Sanitation--Juvenile literature. | Careers--Juvenile literature. | Scenes of crimes--Juvenile literature. | Cleanliness--Juvenile literature. | Refuse and refuse disposal--Juvenile literature.
Classification: DDC 331.70--dc23

TABLE OF CONTENTS

Dirty True Crime Jobs 4

The Dirt. 6

The Work 10

The Clean Up 26

Glossary 30

Online Resources 31

Index 32

DIRTY TRUE CRIME JOBS

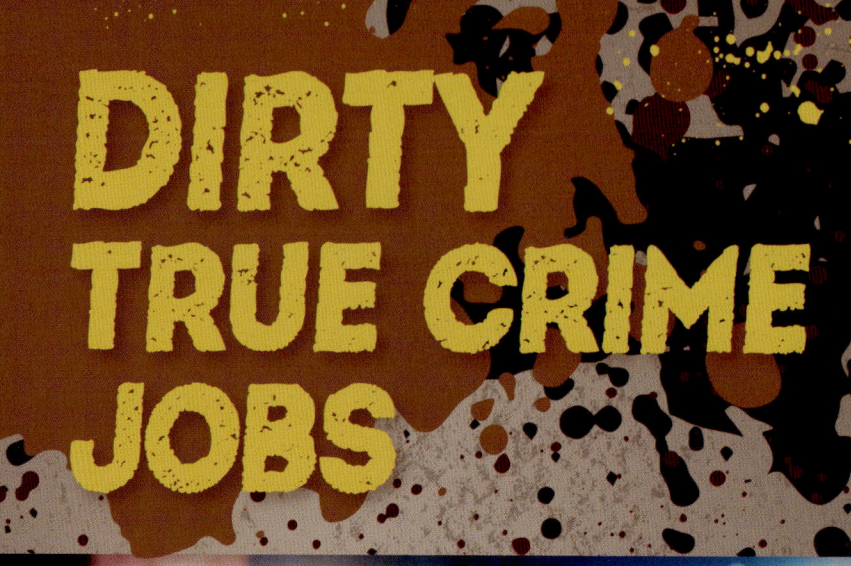

Law enforcement plays a key role in ensuring that criminals face justice. However, investigating the dirtier side of true crime often requires a special kind of person who is willing to take a stab at the truth!

THE DIRT

True crime cases require scientific **accuracy**, a deep understanding of human behavior, and **grit** to solve them.

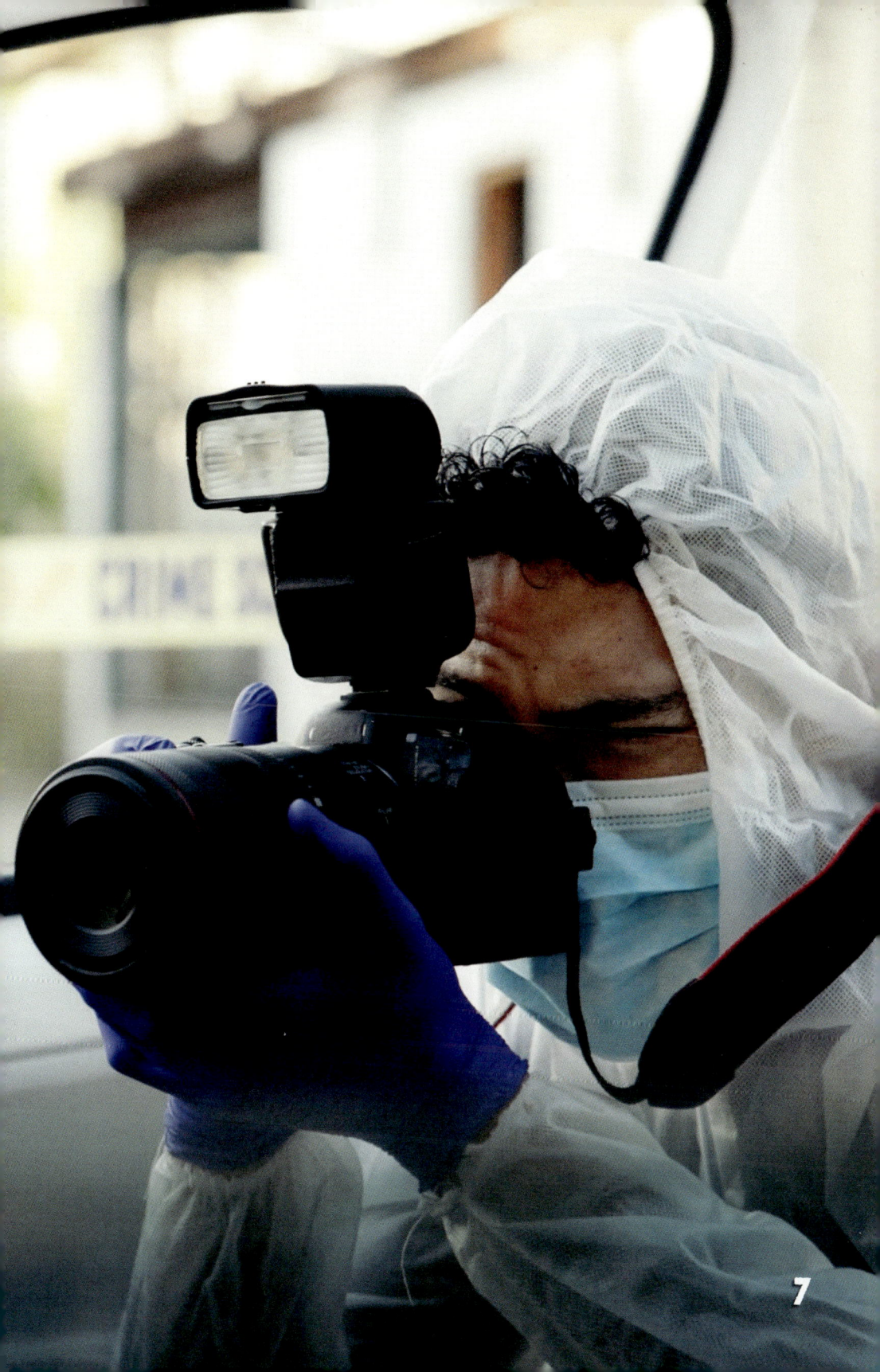

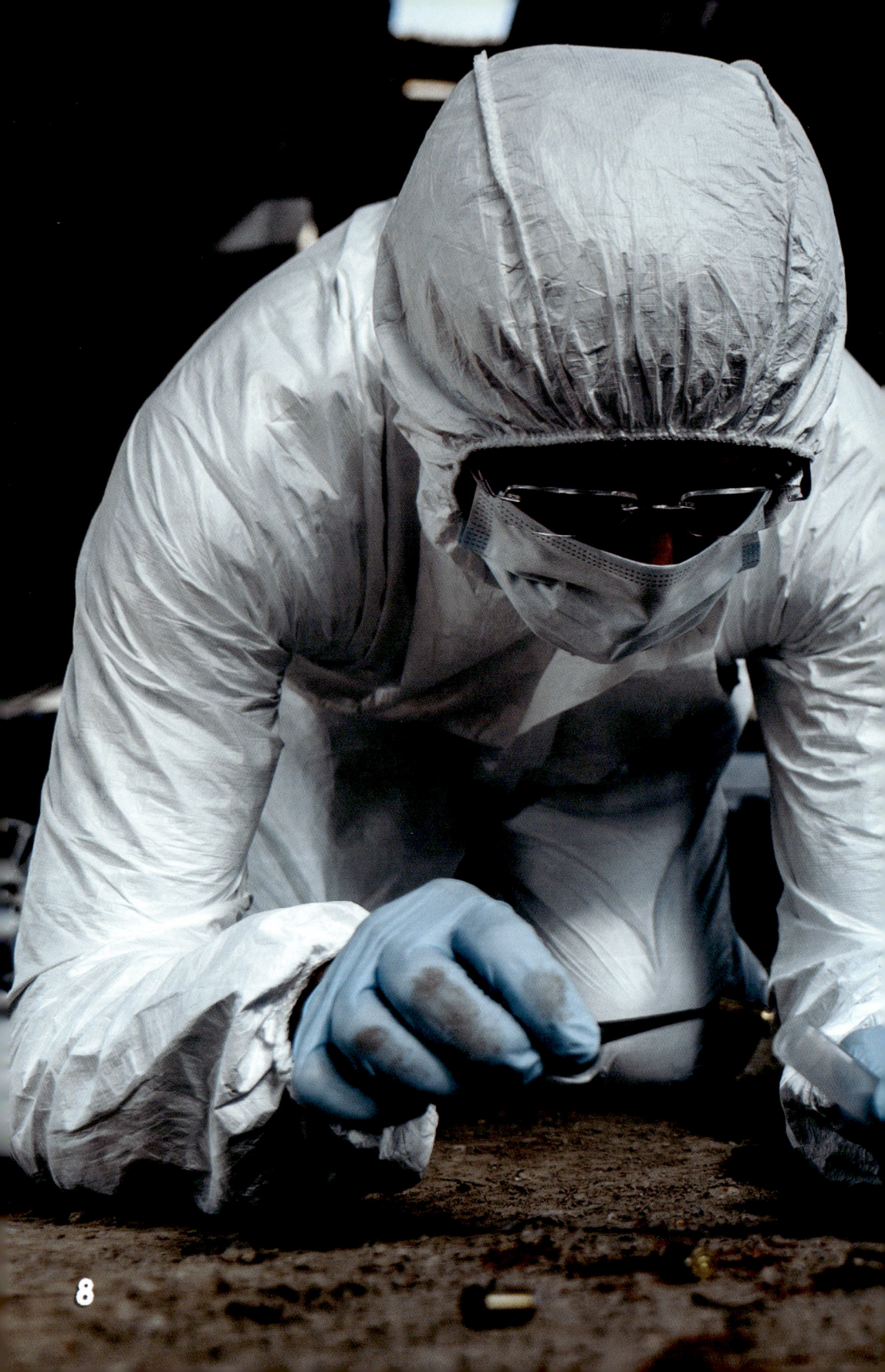

Forensics, underwater recovery, and **arson** investigation jobs can be dirty and unpleasant. However, these jobs are important for delivering justice and keeping our streets clean!

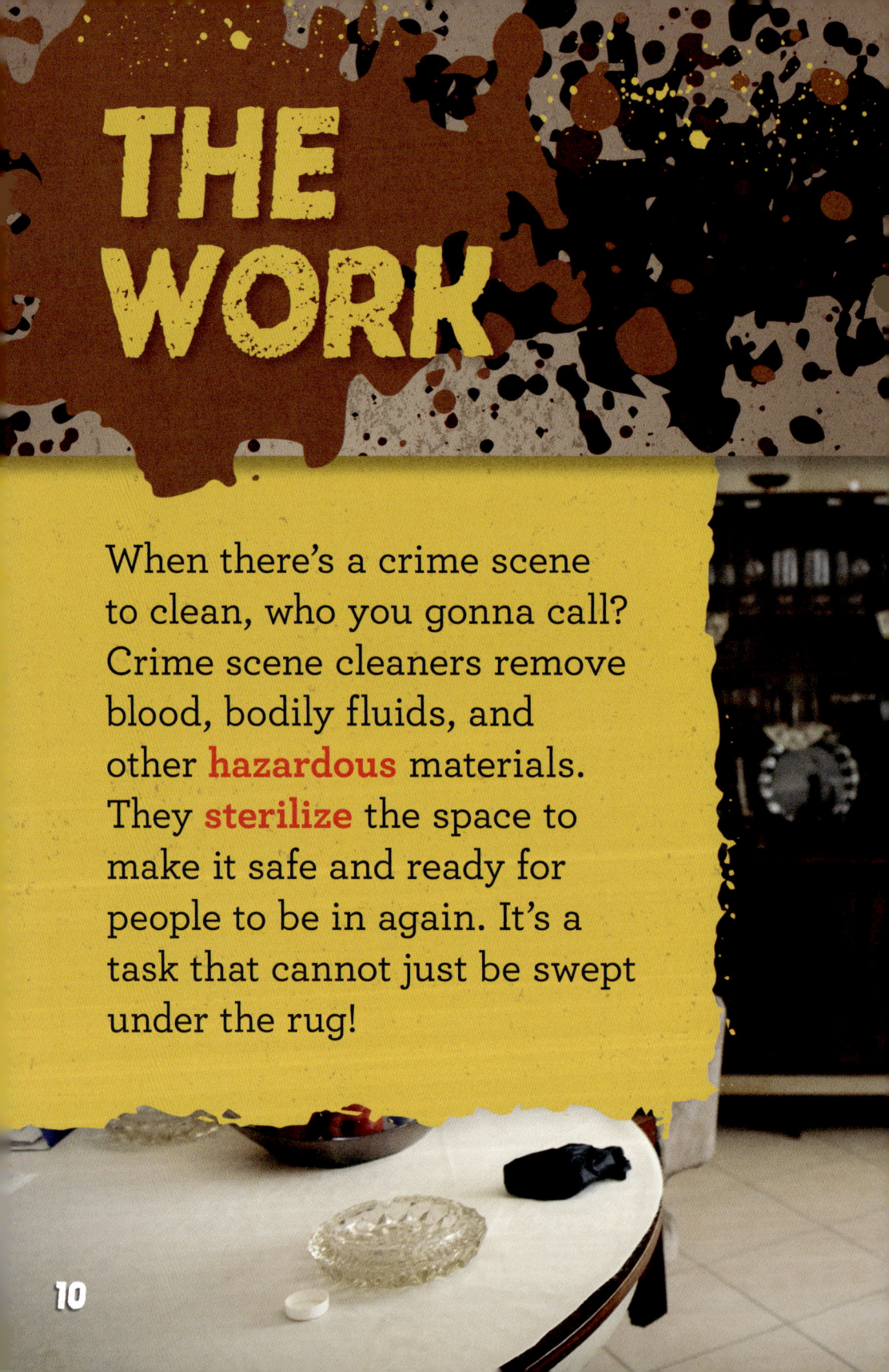

THE WORK

When there's a crime scene to clean, who you gonna call? Crime scene cleaners remove blood, bodily fluids, and other **hazardous** materials. They **sterilize** the space to make it safe and ready for people to be in again. It's a task that cannot just be swept under the rug!

Forensic entomologists are scientists who study the life cycles of insects on dead bodies. Insects can help determine when and how a person died. This job can get creepy and crawly. What these scientists learn is important for solving crimes. Just don't bug them while they work.

Certain dog handlers train dogs to locate missing persons, whether dead or alive. The team operates both outdoors and in collapsed buildings, searching for survivors. The dogs' incredible sense of smell is needed in solving cases. These special pups are man's best friend and a criminal's worst enemy!

Arson investigators determine whether fires were caused accidentally or on purpose. They examine burned materials while studying ash and fumes. The work ensures that those responsible feel the heat of justice on their necks!

Underwater recovery teams look for bodies and clues in lakes, rivers, and oceans. They often work in dark and risky waters and need special skills to dive safely. What they find can help solve crimes and understand accidents, leading to new depths of crime-solving!

Bomb squads handle and dispose of explosive devices. They investigate threats that may be false alarms or potentially fatal.

Squad members wear heavy bomb suits and carefully move through **volatile** situations. The high-risk job is critical to maintaining public safety and ensuring there is no explosive news to report!

Cybercrime **forensic** investigators look at data from digital devices to find online illegal activity. They handle fraud, identity theft, and **hacking** cases. By tracing digital footprints and recovering deleted files, they help computer criminals login to prison!

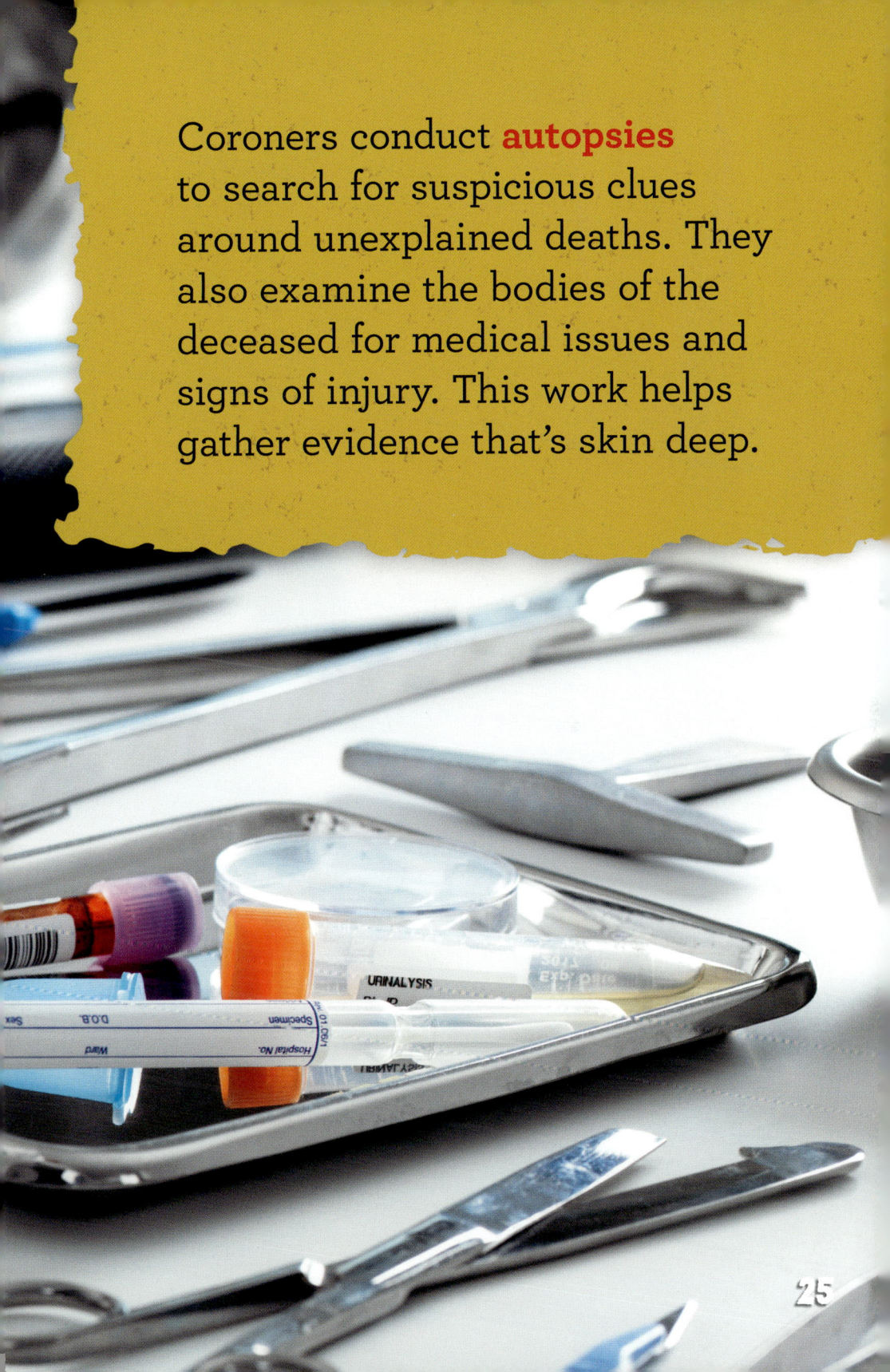

Coroners conduct **autopsies** to search for suspicious clues around unexplained deaths. They also examine the bodies of the deceased for medical issues and signs of injury. This work helps gather evidence that's skin deep.

THE CLEAN UP

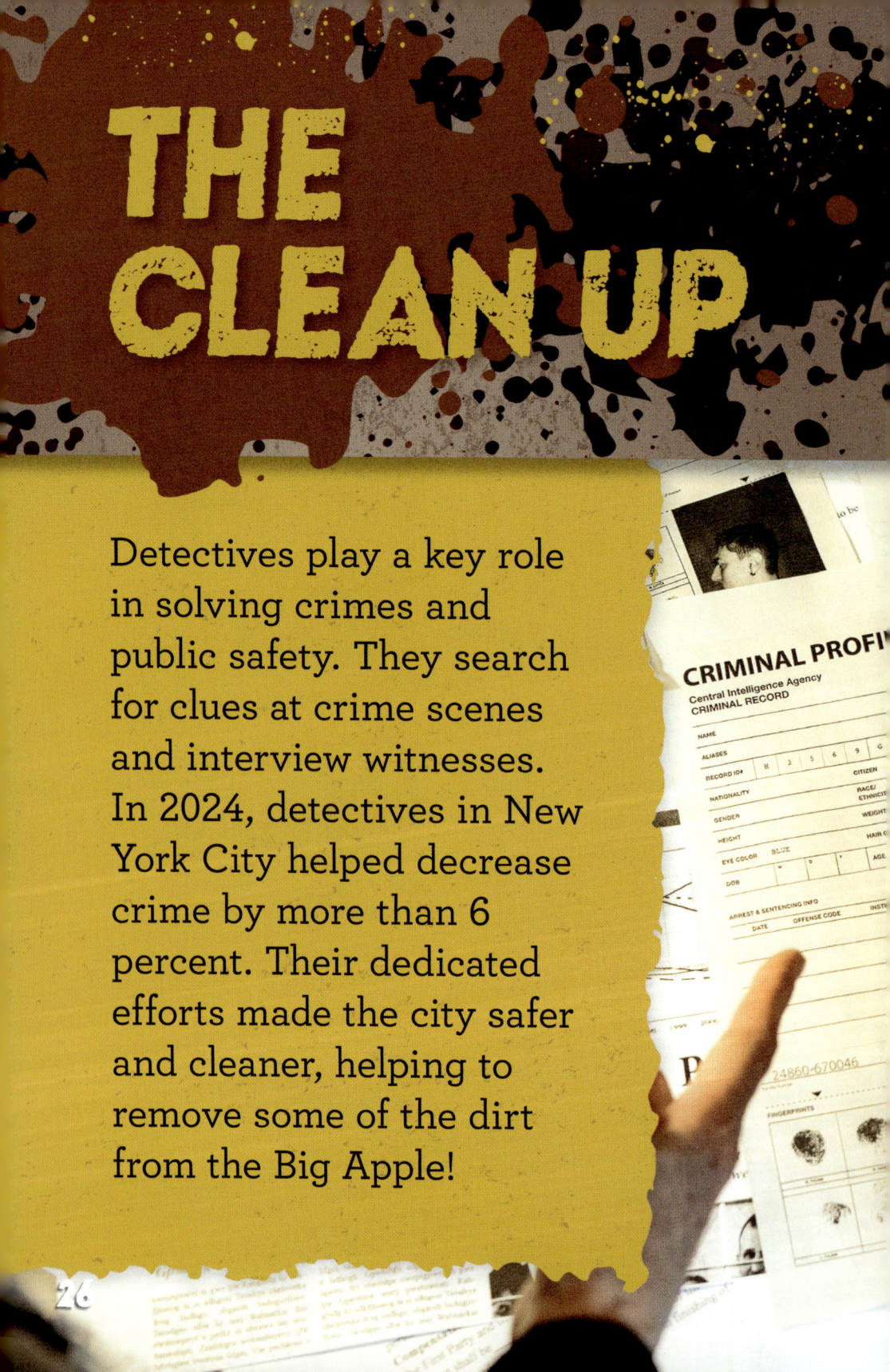

Detectives play a key role in solving crimes and public safety. They search for clues at crime scenes and interview witnesses. In 2024, detectives in New York City helped decrease crime by more than 6 percent. Their dedicated efforts made the city safer and cleaner, helping to remove some of the dirt from the Big Apple!

True crime jobs are tough and intense. The tireless workers explore the darkest parts of their communities to serve up justice without any cop-outs!

GLOSSARY

accuracy – the condition of being free of mistakes or error.

arson – the illegal act of purposefully setting property on fire.

autopsy – a medical examination performed on a deceased individual to determine the time and cause of death.

forensics – the use of scientific methods and techniques in investigating crimes.

grit – toughness of character.

hacking – when a person uses their technical skills to illegally access computer systems and steal information or money from others.

hazardous – full of danger or having many risks.

sterile – free of living germs and bacteria.

volatile – when something can change suddenly and unexpectedly, often for the worse.

ONLINE RESOURCES

Booklinks
NONFICTION NETWORK
FREE! ONLINE NONFICTION RESOURCES

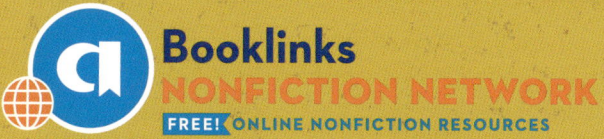

To learn more about true crime jobs, please visit abdobooklinks.com or scan this QR code. These links are routinely monitored and updated to provide the most current information available.

INDEX

arson 9, 16

bomb squads 20, 21

cadaver dogs 15

coroners 25

crime scene cleaning 10

cybercrimes 22

detectives 26

entomology 13

forensic science 9, 13, 22

New York City 26

underwater recovery 9, 18